Welcome to Rainbow Bridge Publishing's Mastering Basic Skills— Grammar series, grade one. Mastering grammar skills builds confidence and enhances a student's entire educational experience. This workbook is designed to help students understand and master sentence construction and fundamental grammatical principles. It both reinforces classroom skills and gets students well on their way to reading and writing independently and competently, and it is ideal for use during or after school.

By making a connection between their previous language experience and the ideas in the text, students realize they have already learned a number of key grammar concepts. Based on NCTE (National Council of Teachers of English) standards and core curriculum, this workbook helps students understand basic sentence patterns, beginning with subject and predicate. They build on this foundation by completing exercises and games that teach proper nouns, plurals, pronouns and verb tense and number. By continually relating workbook concepts to their existing knowledge, students learn to recognize correct grammar and construct their own sentences.

This workbook holds the students' interest with a mix of humor, imagination and instruction. The diverse assignments teach proper use of adjectives and adverbs while also giving students something fun to think about—from dogs to dinosaurs. As students complete the workbook, they will be well prepared to master additional language skills related to word choice, meaning, intent and audience.

Nothing is more basic to a solid education than reading and writing. This workbook helps students enhance both skills, strengthening students' confidence, helping them enjoy language and ultimately encouraging them to read and write on their own.

Rainbow Bridge Publishing
www.summerbridgeactivities.com
www.rbpbooks.com

Table of Contents

Name ____   Date________________

◇ Start Here!

Choose the right subject for each sentence. Write the word.

The <u>subject</u> part of a sentence tells what the sentence is about.

Example: The day begins. <u>Day</u> is the subject.

---

children	doors	ears	chairs
horn	teacher	bell	feet

1. The ___horn___ honks.

2. The _______________ rings.

3. The _______________ yell.

4. The _______________ open.

5. The _______________ run.

6. The _______________ scrape.

7. The _______________ talks.

8. The _______________ listen.

Rob Reasons: What is happening?

Name _________________________________ Date_____________

◇ Start Here!

Circle the subject of each sentence.

1. My (friend) eats snails.

2. Yen eats octopus.

3. Greta eats blue cheese.

4. Pierre eats frog legs.

5. Anna eats oxtail soup.

6. I eat hot dogs.

7. My friends laugh at me.

 Rob Reasons: Can you name a strange food that people eat?

Name _________________________________   Date_____________

◇ Start Here!

Look at the picture and write the word that tells what is happening.

The <u>predicate</u> tells what happens in the sentence.

Example: The dogs run. <u>Run</u> is the predicate.

---

1 Allie 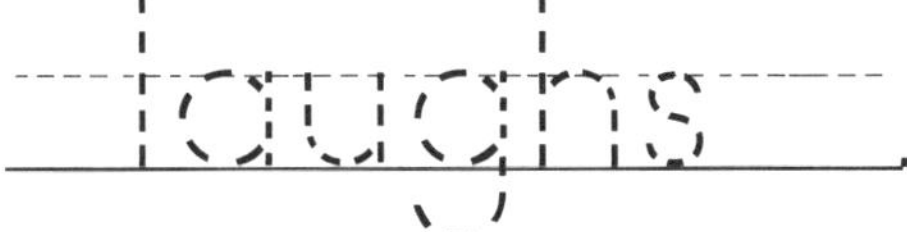 laughs .

2 The clouds  ________________.

3 The seeds  ________________.

4 Tanner 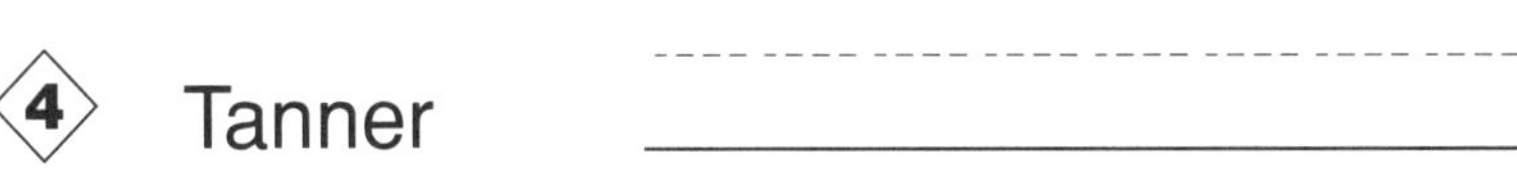 ________________.

5 He 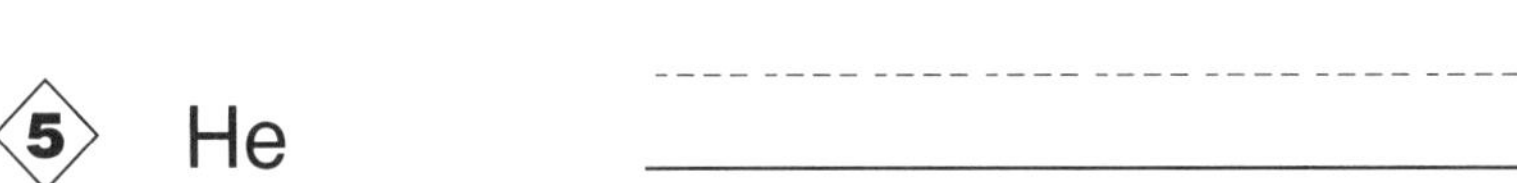 ________________.

 Rob Reasons: Draw what you would grow in your garden.

Name _________________________________ Date_________________

◇ **Start Here!**

Choose the right action word. Write it in the blank.

1. Haley ___walks___ her dog. walks   swims

2. Her dog _____________. oinks   barks

3. The cat _____________. buzzes   meows

4. Haley _____________ with her dog. runs   hops

5. They _____________ in the mud puddle. eat   jump

6. The cat _____________. quacks   purrs

Rob Reasons: On another piece of paper, write what you think the cat was thinking.

Name ____ Date_________________

◇ Start Here!

Draw a fish in the box if the sentence is complete. Draw a circle if it is not.

A <u>sentence</u> is a group of words that tells a complete thought about a person, animal, place, or thing.

1. 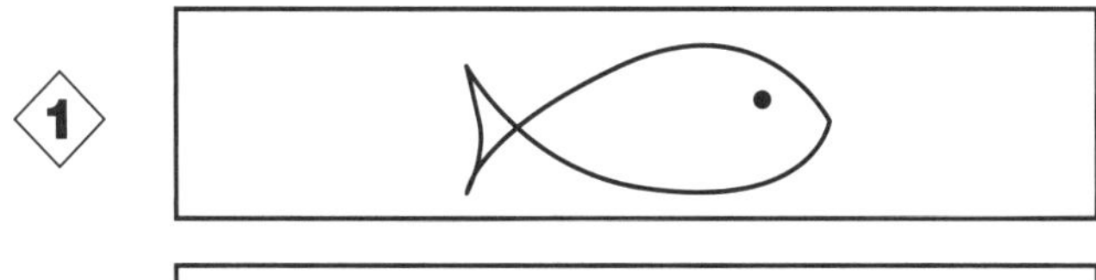 The boat floats.

2.  The fish.

3. One man catches a fish.

4. He throws the fish back.

5.  The lake.

6.  Children swim.

7.  The wind blows.

8.  Cold water.

9.  He rows the boat home.

Name ______________________________________   Date______________________

◇ Start Here!

Write the number of the sentence in the column that tells if it is complete or not complete.

① My mom bakes cookies.

② I eat cookies.

③ Dirty dishes.

④ The crumbs.

⑤ I got sick.

⑥ No cookies.

Complete	Not Complete

Name ____ Date___________________

◇ Start Here!

Write each sentence correctly. Use the code box at the bottom.

Make sure you put a capital letter at the beginning and a period at the end of each sentence. Read what you write out loud. Does it make sense? If the sentence is complete, circle its number.

Example: 1.  the      I see the cat.

---

① U         m+   friend.

____

② U   C.

____

③ The      likes   that   fl+ .

____

④    M   5   y+  +s   old.

____

 = I or y   **R** = are   = can

C = see   **U** = you   **M** = am

= be   **5** = five

The Mixer 

Name _______________________________   Date_______________

◇ Start Here!

Put each mixed-up sentence in order. Read it out loud. Does it make sense?

Remember to start each sentence with a capital letter and end with a period.

Example: mixed cake mom a = Mom mixed a cake.

---

1 oven we it the in put

____

____

2 smells Rob birthday the cake

____

____

3 loves cake he chocolate

____

____

4 took someone candles the off

____

____

5 the ate someone cake

____

____

Rob Reasons: On another piece of paper, write what you think happened.

Fun Sentences

Name ____ Date________________________

◇ Start Here!

Choose one beginning and one ending from each box to make a silly sentence.

Beginnings

The cat climbed	Rob ate	I put bubbles
Cars drive	Our ball rolled	

Endings

on the road.	in the bathtub.	over the sink.
up the tree.	on the TV.	

Example: The cat climbed on the road.

1. ____

2. ____

3. ____

4. ____

5. ____

Rob Reasons: On another piece of paper, see how many more sentences you can make.

Name ____ Date______________

◇ Start Here!

Write a telling sentence about each picture. Remember to begin each sentence with a capital letter and end it with a period.

A <u>telling sentence</u> tells about someone, someplace, or something.

Example: I can fly a kite.

1 ___________________________

2 ___________________________

3 ___________________________

Name ____ Date_____________________

◇ Start Here!
Write a telling sentence about each picture. Remember to begin each one with a capital letter and end it with a period.

1.

2.

3.

   reproducible   www.rbpbooks.com   **MBS—Grammar Grade 1**

Name ____   Date_______________________

◇Start Here!
Choose one word to complete each sentence.

An <u>asking sentence</u> asks about someone, something, or someplace. It often begins with one of the words in the box.

who	what	when	where
why	how	which	

1 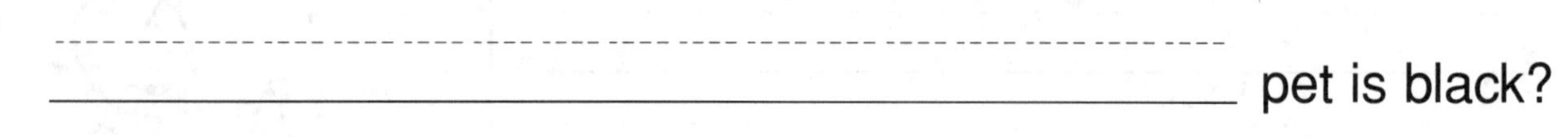 What _______________________ did you draw?

2 _______________________ pet is black?

3 _______________________ are you taking your dog?

4 _______________________ far are you going?

5 _______________________ are you coming home?

Rob Reasons: Some of the sentences have more than one answer. Can you find them?

Name _______________________________________   Date_______________________

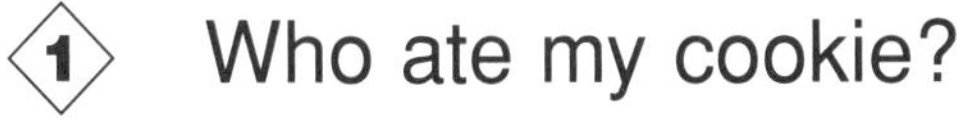

Circle the best asking sentence for each picture.

1   Who ate my cookie?

Where is my sock?

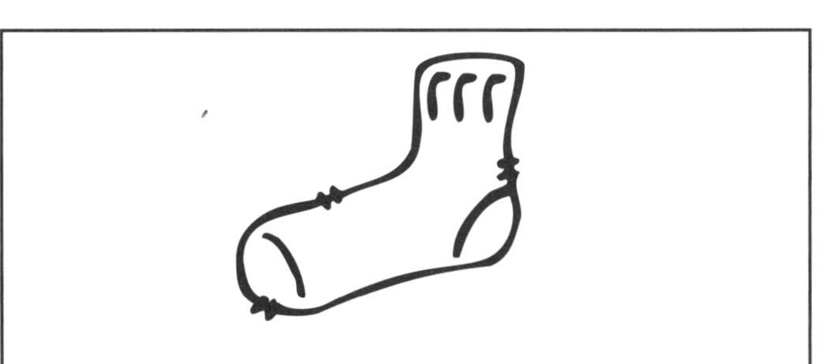

2   What time is it?

Can I have a bite?

3   Will you come to my party?

Why is that on the rug?

4   When do we eat?

Who can run fast?

Name ____   Date_______________

◇ **Start Here!**

Circle the T if it is a telling sentence. Circle the A if it is an asking sentence. Put a period (.) or question mark (?) at the end.

1. A bird made a nest by our door ____   (T)   A

2. Where is it ____   T   A

3. It is in the ivy ____   T   A

4. Look at the eggs ____   T   A

5. How many eggs are there ____   T   A

6. One is hatching ____   T   A

7. Can you see the baby bird ____   T   A

8. Where are its feathers ____   T   A

9. The mother has a worm ____   T   A

Rob Reasons: Look for different nests in your yard. Insects build their nests under leaves and in other places. How many can you find?

What a Blast!  Exclamatory Sentences

Name _______________________________ Date_______________

Read the sentence out loud. Draw a ● mouth if the sentence needs a (!). Draw a ⌐ mouth if it does not.

A sentence that shows you are feeling happy, mad, excited, or afraid ends with an exclamation point (!). These are called <u>exclamatory</u> sentences!

1. I got stung by a bee!

2. Look out for that hole

3. I was asleep

4. My cat had seven kittens

5. That is a big spider

6. Rob watched TV

7. Our class is number one

8. I have a pencil

Name ___________________________________ Date___________________

◇ **Start Here!**

Write a sentence about each picture. Use an exclamation point at the end.

1. ____

2. ____

3. ____

4. ____

Name _________________________________ Date_____________

Color the telling sentences red. Color the asking sentences yellow.
Color the exclamatory sentences green.

I am six years old. I wrote a letter to my pen pal. She wrote one

to me. Her name is Gina. I wrote, "What color is your hair?" She said,

"It is brown." Mine is, too! I wrote, "What color are your eyes?" Hers

are blue. So are mine! I have one sister. She has two brothers. But

they are not as old as we are. We are both six!

Rob Reasons: Write a letter to a friend. Write one telling, one asking,
and one exclamatory sentence.

Name _______________________________________ Date_______________

◇ Start Here!

Circle the T if it is a telling sentence. Circle the A if it is an asking sentence. Circle the E if it is an exclamatory sentence.

1. It is time to start!   T   A   (E)

2. Each person takes a part.   T   A   E

3. The band is marching by.   T   A   E

4. A clown with a horn squirts water in my eye!   T   A   E

5. Where are the horses?   T   A   E

6. They are coming down the street.   T   A   E

7. Don't get too close.   T   A   E

8. They might step on your feet!   T   A   E

9. Who is that waving?   T   A   E

10. I think that is my dad.   T   A   E

11. He is way up on the float!   T   A   E

12. Do you think that he is glad?   T   A   E

Name ____   Date________________________

◇ Start Here!

Circle the nouns that name people.

<u>Nouns</u> are naming words. Some nouns are people-naming words. Circle the people-naming nouns.

Example: The (students) go to school. <u>Students</u> is a people-naming noun.

---

1. The bus driver drives our school bus.

2. Our teacher helps us learn.

3. The principal eats lunch with us.

4. The secretary talks on the intercom.

5. The librarian reads us books.

6. The custodian cleans the floor.

7. The cooks make our lunches.

8. The nurse helps us when we fall.

 Rob Reasons: On another piece of paper, list four of the naming nouns. List more things they do for you.

Name ____   Date_________________

◇**Start Here!**
Write the right noun that names an animal.

Some <u>nouns</u> are animal-naming words. Write in the right animal-naming noun.

panda	mouse	dog	snake
spider	parrots	ants	fish

1. A _____mouse_____ is little and likes cheese.

2. __________________ are busy and make tunnels.

3. __________________ like to swim in water.

4. A __________________ has eight legs.

5. A __________________ is long and has no legs.

6. A __________________ bear comes from China.

7. __________________ can talk like us.

8. My __________________ is spotted and barks a lot.

Rob Reasons: Make a list with your friends of seven animal-naming nouns you have had as pets.

Name ___________________________________   Date__________________

◇ **Start Here!**

Help Rob get home. Draw a line to connect the nouns that name a place.

Some nouns are place-naming words.

Examples: school   home

Name _______________________________ Date_______________

◇ Start Here!
Color in the pictures that name things.

Some <u>nouns</u> are thing-naming words.

Examples: rock   scissors   paper

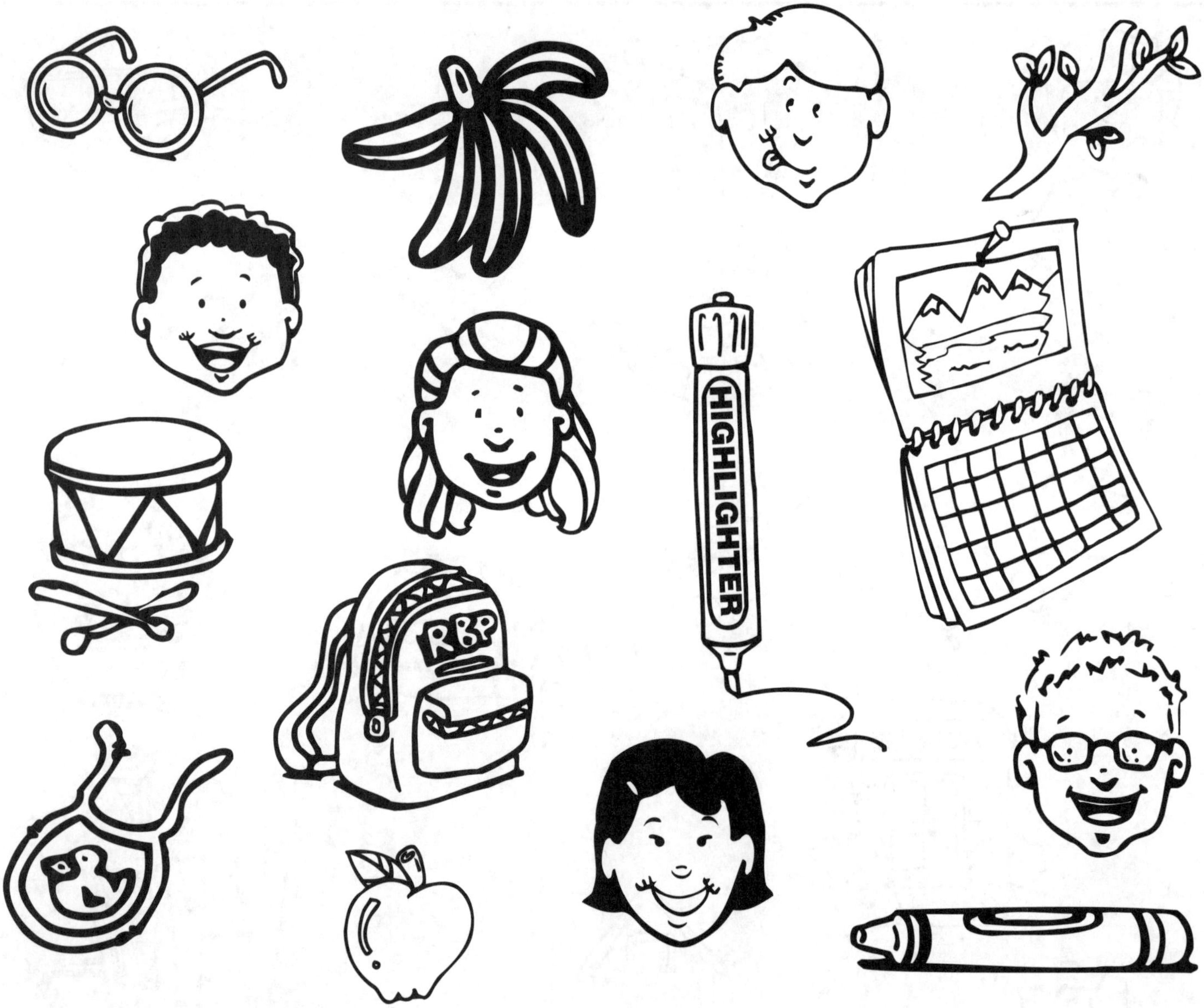

Rob Reasons: What are some things you might see from a spaceship? Draw them.

Name ____ Date____________________

◇ Start Here!

Color the nouns in this story.

1 My brother found a lost dog at the school. Mom says the dog

found my brother George!

The dog is a puppy and looks like a rag. My little sister yells,

"Rags!" and the puppy comes.

Our family put an ad in the newspaper. Not one person called.

We have a dog now. Mom says our dog eats like a horse. But Rags

eats dog food, not hay.

Rob Reasons: Write a story telling what would happen if you found a lost pet.

Name _______________________________________   Date_______________

◇**Start Here!**
Fill in the blanks with proper nouns you know.

Some nouns are special names of people, animals, places and things. These are called <u>proper</u> <u>nouns</u>. They begin with a capital letter.

Example: Mrs. Landry teaches me piano. <u>Mrs.</u> <u>Landry</u> is the proper noun.

1. _Mrs. Ross_______________ also plays the piano.

2. ______________________________ shops at the store.

3. ______________________________ is a nice cat.

4. ______________________________ is our teacher.

5. I live on ______________________ Street.

6. My friend lives on ______________________ Street.

7. She is going home to watch ______________________ on TV.

Rob Reasons: Cut out some special names from a magazine. Write some sentences like those above. Glue the special names in the blanks.

Make a Choice 

Name _______________________________   **Date**_______________

◇ **Start Here!**

Choose one word from the Proper Nouns box and one from the Nouns box to complete each sentence. Use each word only one time.

Proper Nouns

Rockridge   Mrs. Tenny   Oreos®   McDonald's®

Nouns

umbrella   card   sack   cookies

1 The wet _umbrella_ was found at _______________

Elementary.

2 _______________ are my favorite _______________ to eat.

3 We ate a _______________ of fries at _______________ .

4 _______________ sent me a _______________ .

Rob Reasons: Make a proper nouns column and a nouns column. See how many you can think of to list.

Name ____ Date_______________

◇ Start Here!

Fill in the blanks with one of the pronouns in the box. Use each word only once.

<u>Pronouns</u> are words like <u>I</u>, <u>me</u>, <u>you</u>, <u>she</u>, <u>he</u>, <u>it</u>, <u>they</u> and <u>we</u> that can take the place of names in a sentence.

I	he	they
me	she	it	we

My class went to the zoo. The zookeeper said giraffes are tall.

He said ____________ can be 16 feet high. ____________

____________ saw the mother giraffe feeding her baby boy. ____________ is called

a cow and ____________ is called a calf. Most giraffes live in Africa.

____________ is very hot there. A giraffe can go four weeks without a

drink. That makes ____________ thirsty just to think about it!

Name ____ Date_______________

◇ Start Here!

Write a pronoun for each sentence. Put it in the right place in the crossword puzzle.

Down

1. The thunder made a huge bang.   <u>It</u> made a huge bang.

2. My friends and I saw the lightning.

4. My dad told us to go into the car.

Across

3. All our neighbors watched from inside their homes.

Rob Reasons: Ask your parents for some rules to follow during a storm. Write them down and put them by the phone.

Name _______________________________ Date_______________

◇ Start Here!
Color in the right circle for each sentence. Read each sentence out loud to see if it sounds right.

1 ________I________ like to play baseball. (**I**) (me)

2 The pitcher throws __________ the ball. (I) (me)

3 Sometimes __________ catch it. (I) (me)

4 Sometimes __________ hit it. (I) (me)

5 Sometimes they tag __________ out. (I) (me)

6 __________ like to run fast to home plate. (I) (me)

7 The coach gives __________ a high five. (I) (me)

8 __________ helped our team win! (I) (me)

Rob Reasons: Write a sentence using I. Write a sentence using me.

Paint Me a Picture 

Name ____ Date_______________

◇ Start Here!

Put the nouns that name only one in the red brush. Put the other words in the blues brush.

Some nouns name only one person, animal, place or thing. Other nouns name more than one. These are called <u>plural</u> <u>nouns</u>.

Example: <u>Boy</u> names one thing. <u>Boys</u> names more than one thing.

| purple | reds | green | yellow |
| blacks | blues | white | orange |

Red Brush

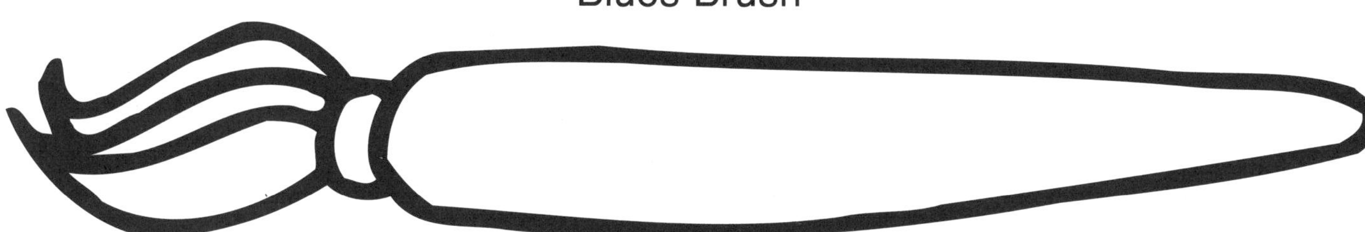

Blues Brush

Rob Reasons: Find out what is the world's tallest building, tree, or person.

Name ___________________________________   Date_______________

◇ Start Here!

Add <u>s</u> to the nouns below to show more than one. Write the word in the blank.

For some nouns that name more than one person, animal, place, or thing, add an <u>s</u> at the end.

1. Some _spiders_ are bigger than your hand and eat birds.
   (spider)

2. Gecko _______________ can walk upside down on the ceiling.
   (lizard)

3. Tree _______________ are so light they can sit on a leaf.
   (frog)

4. Some _______________ eat sand.
   (worm)

5. _______________ make honey and sting.
   (bee)

6. Some _______________ can hide on twigs by holding very still.
   (insect)

7. _______________ sleep upside down.
   (bat)

Name _________________________________   Date_________________________

 **◇Start Here!**
Choose the noun that matches each picture. Write it in the blank.

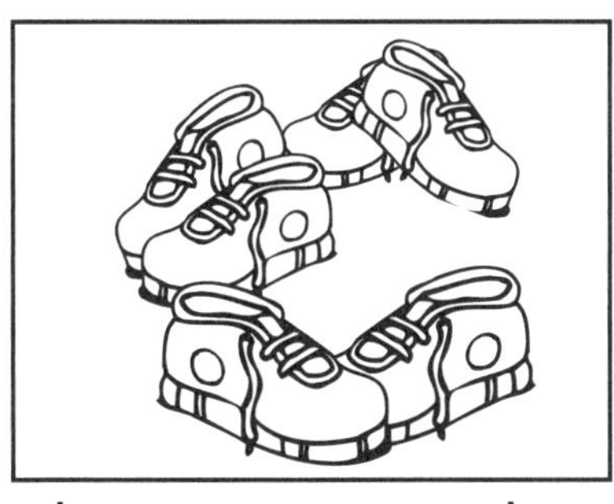

1. shoes   shoe

shoes

2. sock   socks

3. sweater   sweaters

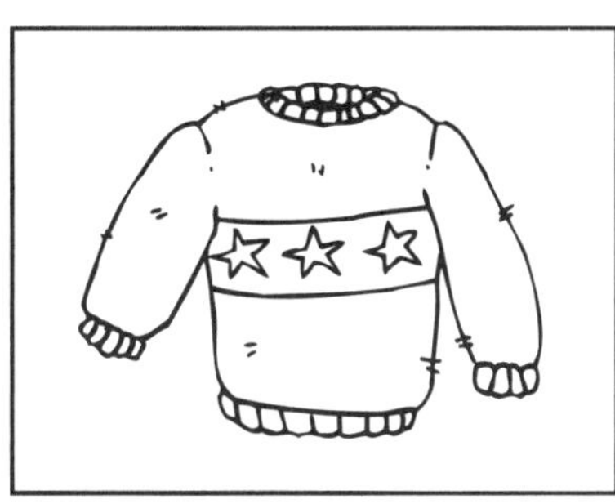

4. hats   hat

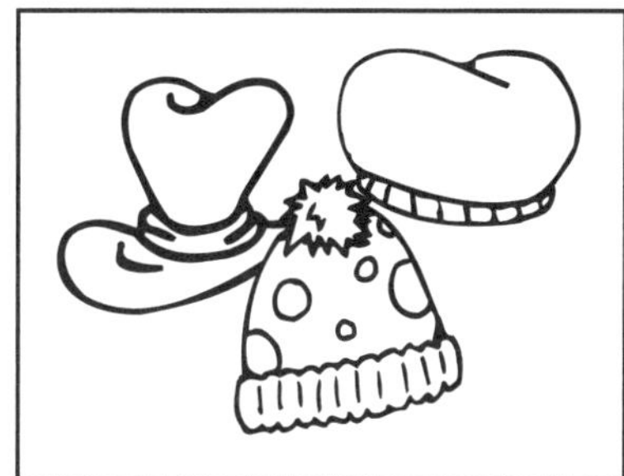

Draw a picture that shows each word.

5.

toys

6.

dress

Name ___________________________________ Date _______________

◇ Start Here!

Circle the verb in each sentence.

A <u>verb</u> is an action word. Action words tell what a person or an animal does.

Examples: The students run. <u>Run</u> is the action verb.

---

1 Some squirrels fly.

2 Some monkeys howl.

3 Some fish crawl out of water onto tree roots.

4 A newborn kangaroo climbs into its mother's pouch.

5 Koala bears eat one kind of leaf.

6 Some eagles fish.

7 Some fish carry their babies in their mouths.

Rob Reasons: Look for more strange actions some animals do. Write them down.

Hats!

Name ____ Date_________________________

◇ Start Here!

Write three action words (verbs) in each hat that tell what the naming words (nouns) can do.

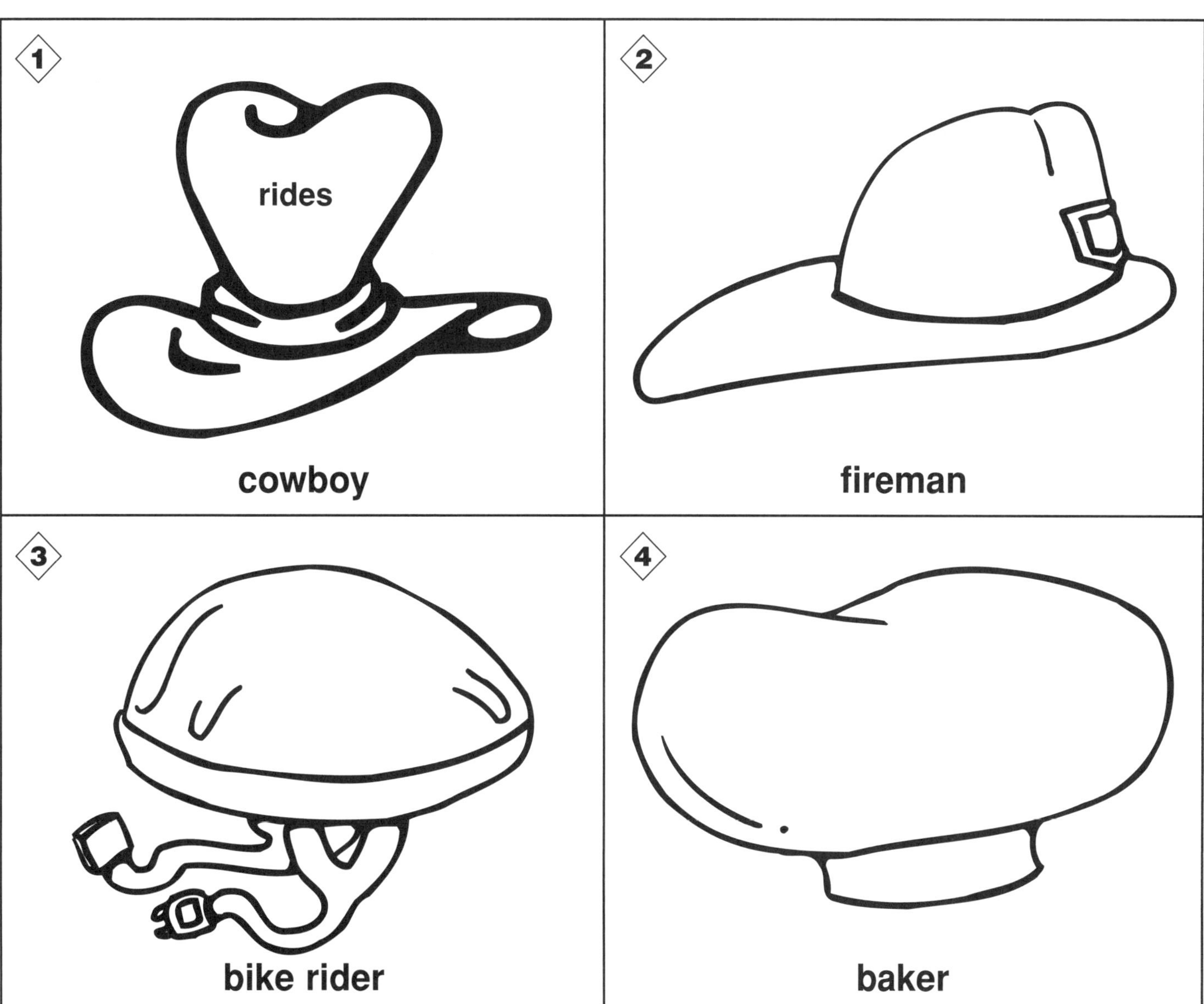

Rob Reasons: Write a sentence about your favorite person. Use some of the verbs you put in the hats.

 reproducible   www.rbpbooks.com   **MBS—Grammar Grade 1**

Name _________________________________   Date_______________

◇ **Start Here!**
Match the picture with the right action word. Color each picture.

dig

sing

fly

swim

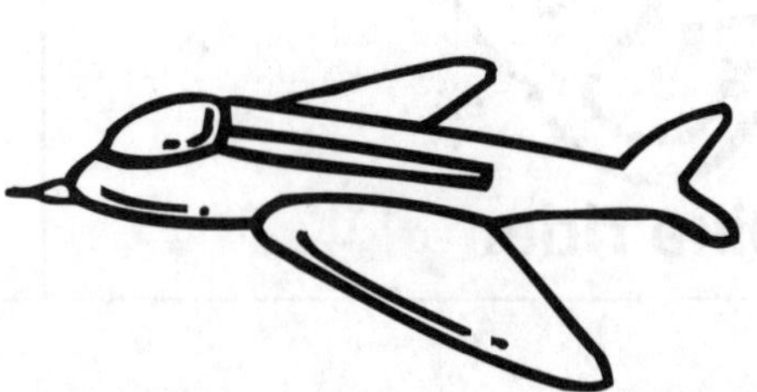

eat

Rob Reasons: Draw a picture that shows a person, animal, and thing doing the same action. Write a sentence using the action word.

Name ____   Date_________________

◇Start Here!

Circle the correct linking verb. Write in the blank.

<u>Is</u> and <u>are</u> are two <u>linking verbs</u>. They tell about something that is happening now.

1   My sister Carlie and I _____are_____ going sledding.   is   (are)

2   Carlie __________ two years older than I.   is   are

3   We __________ taking turns on the sled.   is   are

4   My friend Shelly yells. She __________ scared.   is   are

5   Shelly __________ riding with us.   is   are

6   The three of us __________ going very fast.   is   are

7   Look out! We __________ going . . .   is   are

____

____

Rob Reasons: Finish sentence 7 with what you think might happen.

Name _______________________________ Date_______________

◇Start Here!
Circle the correct linking verbs.

Some <u>linking verbs</u> tell about the past.

1. Dinosaurs was/were alive millions of years ago.

2. One dinosaur was/were one of the biggest animals that ever lived.

3. Some of them was/were flying reptiles.

4. Most dinosaurs was/were egg layers.

5. The first kind of horse was/were a dinosaur.

6. It was/were only about one foot tall.

7. I wish dinosaurs was/were still alive!

Rob Reasons: What dinosaur do you wish was still alive? Why?

Name _______________________ Date _______________

◇Start Here!

Take away the <u>s</u> and add <u>ed</u> to these verbs. Write the verb.

Some <u>verbs</u> tell what happened in the past.

1. Jill <u>plays</u> with her marbles on the hill. _played_

2. The cat's eye <u>rolls</u> into a can. ______________

3. Jack <u>skates</u> around some. ______________

4. He <u>picks</u> up the steelies. ______________

5. A car <u>cracks</u> the crystal one. ______________

6. Jill <u>crawls</u> under a wagon for her striped one. ______________

7. Jack <u>saves</u> the day by catching the rest in a net. ______________

Rob Reasons: Find more about the 2,000-year-old sport of marbles by looking in an encyclopedia.

Name ____   Date ______________

◇Start Here!
Add <u>ed</u> to the underlined verbs. Write the past-tense verb underneath.

1. Rabbits <u>jump</u> and <u>rush</u> around.

   jumped

2. The cats just <u>lick</u> their fur.

3. The mice <u>peek</u> out without a sound.

4. Some dogs just <u>growl</u> and snarl.

5. The parrots <u>talk</u>, the owners <u>walk</u>.

6. And when things <u>start</u> the curtains <u>part</u>.

7. The pets <u>show</u> off their ribbons.

Name ____ Date___________________

◇ **Start Here!**
Draw and color a picture of the sentences below. The adjectives (describing words) are underlined.

Some words describe. They are called <u>adjectives</u>. Adjectives tell how peo-ple, animals, things, or places look, feel, taste, smell, or sound. Sometimes you can ask "What kind?" about the noun to help you find the describing word.

Example: I have a nice friend. What kind of friend is he? <u>Nice</u> is an adjective.

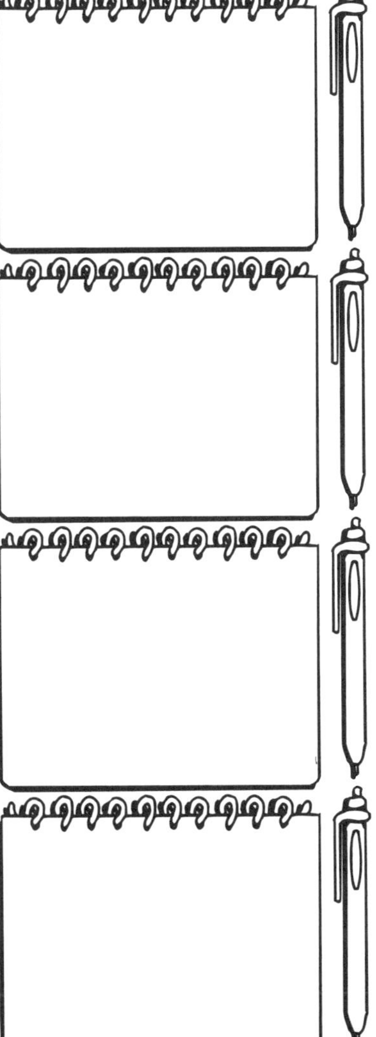

1 The <u>red</u> balloon had <u>green</u> stripes.

2 The chair was <u>pink</u> and <u>yellow</u>.

3 The <u>short</u> girl had <u>black</u> hair.

4 My <u>big</u> house is <u>brown</u>.

 reproducible   www.rbpbooks.com   **MBS—Grammar Grade 1**

Name ____   Date_____________________

◇ Start Here!
Make an X on the describing words (adjectives). Then think of one
more word that describes the underlined word. Write it.

Examples: I love hot <u>bread</u> with butter.   white

---

1 We order spicy <u>chicken</u>. ________ crispy ________

2 My mom pours me cold <u>milk</u>. _______________________

3 Renny got a handful of my salty <u>potato</u> <u>chips</u>. _______________

4 For a snack I like crunchy <u>celery</u>. _______________

5 At the park we buy sour <u>lemonade</u>. _______________

6 I helped spread thick <u>icing</u> on brownies. _______________

Name ____ Date_______________

◇ Start Here!

Write the naming words (nouns) from the word box next to the describing words (adjectives).

| head | hands | eyes | stomach |
| ears | feet | legs | |

1. ringing, listening _______ears_______

2. clapping, waving ____________________

3. hungry, growling ____________________

4. tapping, kicking ____________________

5. sleepy, blinking ____________________

6. running, walking ____________________

7. thinking, turning ____________________

Rob Reasons: On another piece of paper, write five more describing words (adjectives) that tell about your body or a part of it.

Up or Down?

Name _______________________ Date_______________

◇ Start Here!

Color in the dot by the word that tells what is happening.

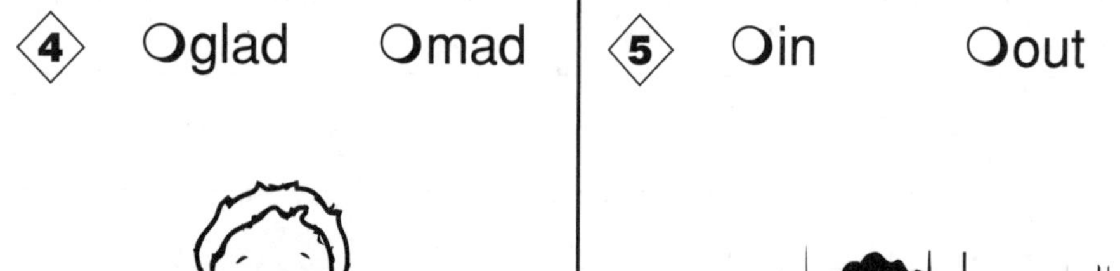

Rob Reasons: Write a story that tells what happened in the pictures. Use some of the words.

Name ____　Date________________

◇ Start Here!

Read the underlined word. Choose an opposite word from the word box, write the new word in the blank sentence.

glad	awake	new	next to	always

1 I am <u>sad</u> my friend Jenny is moving.　______________________

2 I was <u>asleep</u> when her family moved.　______________________

3 Now they have a very <u>old</u> house.　______________________

4 It is <u>far away from</u> mine.　______________________

5 We <u>never</u> see each other now!　______________________

Rob Reasons: Which ending do you like best? Why?

Name ___________________________________ Date_______________

◇ Start Here!

Read the words in the word box. They show ownership. Read the story. Draw a circle around each possessive word.

<u>Possessives</u> are words that tell who owns something.

her	his	mine	our
their	my	its	your

Myron and Monica are twins.

"I will take away your ball if you don't share."

Look, their ball is losing its air!

Monica gets her pump. Myron gets his patch.

"Look, Mom. Our ball is fixed!"

Answer Pages

Page 3
1. horn
2. bell
3. children
4. doors
5. feet
6. chairs
7. teacher
8. ears

Page 4
1. friend
2. Yen
3. Greta
4. Pierre
5. Anna
6. I
7. friends

Page 5
1. laughs
2. rain
3. grow
4. eats
5. digs

Page 6
1. walks
2. barks
3. meows
4. runs
5. jump
6. purrs

Page 7
1. (fish)
2. 0
3. (fish)
4. (fish)
5. 0
6. (fish)
7. (fish)
8. 0
9. (fish)

Page 8
Complete
1, 2, 5
Not Complete
3, 4, 6

Page 9
1. You can be my friend.
2. You see.
3. The frog likes that fly.
4. I am five years old.
[circled 1, 3, 4]

Page 10
1. We put it in the oven.
2. Rob smells the birthday cake.
3. He loves chocolate cake.
4. Someone took the candies off.
5. Someone ate the cake.

Page 11
Answers will vary.

Page 12
Answers will vary.

Page 13
Answers will vary.

Page 14
1. what or who
2. which or what
3. where or why
4. how
5. when, why or how

Page 15
1. Where is my sock?
2. Can I have a bite?
3. Will you come to my party?
4. When do we eat?

Page 16
1. ., T　　2. ?, A　　3. ., T
4. ., T　　5. ?, A　　6. ., T
7. ?, A　　8. ?, A　　9. ., T

Page 17
1. (filled) mouth　　2. (filled) mouth
3. (straight) mouth　　4. (filled) mouth
5. (filled) mouth　　6. (straight) mouth
7. (filled) mouth　　8. (straight) mouth

Page 18
Answers will vary.

Page 19
Telling-red
I am six years old.
I wrote a letter to my pen pal.
She wrote one to me.
Her name is Gina.
She said, "It is brown."
Hers are blue.
I have one sister.
She has two brothers.
But they are not as old as we are.
Asking-yellow
What color is your hair?
What color are your eyes?
Exclamatory-green
Mine is, too!
So are mine!
We are both six!

Page 20
1. E　　2. T　　3. T
4. E　　5. A　　6. T
7. T　　8. E　　9. A
10. T　　11. E　　12. A

Page 21
1. bus driver
2. teacher
3. principal
4. secretary
5. librarian
6. custodian
7. cooks
8. nurse

Page 22
1. mouse
2. ants
3. fish
4. spider
5. snake
6. panda
7. parrots
8. dog

Page 23
Line from Rob to:
school
mountains
home
igloo
store
barn

Answer Pages

Page 24
Words colored in:
glasses
bananas
twig
drum
pen
pack
calendar
bib
apple
crayon

Page 25
Nouns colored:
brother
dog
school
Mom
dog
brother
dog
puppy
rag
sister
puppy
family
ad
newspaper
person
dog
Mom
horse
dog food
hay

Page 26
Answers will vary.

Page 27
1. umbrella, Rockridge
2. Oreos®, cookie
3. sack, McDonald's®
4. Mrs. Tenny, card

Page 28
He
they
We
She
he
It
me

Page 29
Down
1. it
2. we
4. he
Across
3. they

Page 30
1. I   2. me   3. I
4. I   5. me   6. I
7. me   8. I

Page 31
Red Brush
purple
white
green
yellow
orange
Blues Brush
reds
blacks
blues

Page 32
1. spiders
2. lizards
3. frogs
4. worms
5. bees
6. insects
7. bats

Page 33
shoes, sock, sweater, hats
Pictures will vary, but the first square
should have more than one toy. The
second should have one dress.

Page 34
1. fly   2. howl   3. crawl
4. climbs   5. eat   6. fish
7. carry

Page 35
Answers will vary.

Page 36
The child draws a path to the correct
word.
dig   swim   sing
eat   fly

Page 37
1. are   2. is   3. are
4. is   5. is   6. are
7. are

Page 38
1. were   2. was   3. were
4. were   5. was   6. was
7. were

Page 39
1. played   2. rolled   3. skated
4. picked   5. cracked   6. crawled
7. saved

Page 40
1. jumped, rushed
2. licked
3. peeked
4. growled
5. talked, walked
6. started, parted
7. showed

Page 41
Drawings will vary.

Page 42
X-ed words
1. Spicy   2. cold   3. salty
4. crunchy   5. sour   6. thick
Answers will vary.

Page 43
1. ears   2. hands   3. stomach
4. feet   5. eyes   6. legs
7. head

Page 44
1. new   2. on   3. up
4. glad   5. out

Page 45
1. glad   2. awake   3. new
4. next to   5. always

Page 46
Circles around:
my   mine   your
their   its   her
his   our

Rainbow Bridge Publishing
Certificate
of Completion

Awarded to

____

for the completion of

Mastering Basic Skills

_______________________   _______________________
Publisher's Signature   Parent's Signature

Receive RBP's FREE Parent and Teacher on-line newsletter!

Receive special offers, FREE learning exercises and great ideas to use in your classroom and at home!

To receive our on-line newsletter, please provide us with the following information:

Name: _______________________

Address: _______________________

City: _______ State: ___ Zip: _______

Email Address: _______________________

Store where book was purchased: _______________________

Child's grade level: _______________________

Book title purchased: _______________________

Or visit our website:

www.sbakids.com

Or Call:
801-268-8887

Summer Bridge Activities™

Title	Price
Grade P-K	$12.95
Grade K-1	$12.95
Grade 1-2	$12.95
Grade 2-3	$12.95
Grade 3-4	$12.95
Grade 4-5	$12.95
Grade 5-6	$12.95

Summer Bridge Middle School™

Title	Price
Grade 6-7	$12.95
Grade 7-8	$12.95

Summer Bridge Reading Activities™

Title	Price
Grade 1-2	$6.95
Grade 2-3	$6.95
Grade 3-4	$6.95

Summer Journal™

Title	Price
Summer Journal™	$4.95

Summer Dailies™

Title	Price
Summer Dailies™	$4.95

Summer Traveler™

Title	Price
Summer Traveler™	$4.95

Math Bridge™

Title	Price
Grade 1	$9.95
Grade 2	$9.95
Grade 3	$9.95
Grade 4	$9.95
Grade 5	$9.95
Grade 6	$9.95
Grade 7	$9.95
Grade 8	$9.95

Reading Bridge™

Title	Price
Grade 1	$9.95
Grade 2	$9.95
Grade 3	$9.95
Grade 4	$9.95
Grade 5	$9.95
Grade 6	$9.95
Grade 7	$9.95
Grade 8	$9.95

Skill Builders™

Title	Price
Phonics Grade 1	$2.50
Spelling Grade 2	$2.50
Vocabulary Grade 3	$2.50
Reading Grade 1	$2.50
Reading Grade 2	$2.50
Reading Grade 3	$2.50
Math Grade 1	$2.50
Math Grade 2	$2.50
Math Grade 3	$2.50
Subtraction Grade 1	$2.50
Subtraction Grade 2	$2.50
Multiplication Grade 3	$2.50

Connection Series™

Title	Price
Reading Grade 1	$10.95
Reading Grade 2	$10.95
Reading Grade 3	$10.95
Math Grade 1	$10.95
Math Grade 2	$10.95
Math Grade 3	$10.95

Mastering Basic Skills™

Title	Price
Grammar Grade 1	$5.95
Grammar Grade 2	$5.95
Grammar Grade 3	$5.95
Word Problems Grade 1	$4.95
Word Problems Grade 2	$4.95
Word Problems Grade 3	$4.95
Word Problems Grade 4	$4.95
Listening Skills Grade 1	$4.95
Listening Skills Grade 2	$4.95
Listening Skills Grade 3	$4.95

Math Test Preparation™

Title	Price
Math Test Prep Grade 1	$10.95
Math Test Prep Grade 2	$10.95
Math Test Prep Grade 3	$10.95

First Step Spanish™

Title	Price
Colors/Shapes	$5.95
Alphabet/Numbers	$5.95

Available everywhere!
Visit your favorite bookstore.

Place
Proper
Postage
Here

Rainbow Bridge Publishing
PO Box 571470
Salt Lake City, Utah 84157

Keeping Children Busy, Happy, and Learning During the Summer and Beyond!